Argument by Design

Argument by Design

Katherine Smith

Washingto

Copyright ©2003 by Katherine Smith

Acknowledgments

Grateful thanks to the following journals and reviews in which some of these poems first appeared: *Clockwatch Review, Hawaii Pacific Review, Illuminations, Kalliope, The Laurel Review, The Ledge, The Lucid Stone, Many Mountains Moving, Natural Bridge, New Millennium Writings, Now & Then, Poetry ("Belleville"), Petroglyph, Shenandoah, Smartish Pace, Snake Nation Review,* and *The Southern Review.*

The author also wishes to express her gratitude to her teachers, particularly to Marilyn Kallet.

Thanks for the careful reading of this manuscript, or of parts of it, to Linda Parsons Marion, Jeff Daniel Marion, Jane Satterfield, Margaret Weaver, Judy Loest, and Jeff Hardin. Thanks also to Sid Gold and the members of the Washington Writers' Publishing House, and to Bernie Jankowski for the book design.

Finally, fellowships to the Virginia Center for the Creative Arts and the Mary Anderson Center for the Arts enabled me to complete this book.

Cover photograph © Hans Jürg Kupper, Basel/Switzerland. Collection: Frac, Fonds Régional d'Art Contemporain d'Ile-de-France, Paris

Photograph of Katherine Smith by R. Wilson.

Library of Congress Cataloguing-in-Publication Data

Smith, Katherine, 1960-
  Argument by Design / Katherine Smith.
    p. cm.
  ISBN 0-931846-69-2 (alk. paper)
  I. Title.
  PS3619.M589A74 2003
  811'.6--dc22

                                2003060125

Washington Writers' Publishing House
P.O. Box 15271
Washington, D.C. 20003

For my parents and for my daughter, Justina Maria Stokes

Table of Contents

I

II

III

O que poderia ter sido, o que deveria ter havido, o que a Lei ou a Sorte não deram — atirei-os às mancheias para a alma do homem e ella perturbou-se de sentir a vida viva do que não existe.

What could have been, what should have existed, what law or Fate don't offer, I hurled by the armful into the soul of humankind, into a soul ever since disturbed by the living life of what doesn't exist.

The Devil's Hour

— Fernando Pessoa

I

HARVEST

Stacked pyramids of the equinoctial
   fruit ripened in the Place des Fêtes, sweet pith
whose seed sprouts memory. We wandered the real
   as if under the spell of some good witch,
pomegranates like runes measured into our baskets
   once fat with berries, peaches, plums. From
tattered wicker I extrapolate
   what else was there: the voluminous crumb
of our marriage stained with a wine
   so sweet it numbed us to the end, betrayal
we cooked like a tumbling heap of Jerusalem
   artichokes, those bitter, twisted vegetables
we loved to eat dripping with butter-soaked
   onions, with greasy chunks of russet apple.

BLACKBIRDS

On our way to ruins we stumbled
over buried roots, up a rocky hill, then round
and round the winding stairs until, at the top,
we saw what we'd come for: green pastures
rolling into the misty distance, Paris sparkling
on the horizon like a dream, lime willows
stroking the crooked river like thin hands,
the safety we sought in marriage blown
like steam from our tea that afternoon
in the dark café. Like the paintings
of Christ hung carelessly in museum corners
the milori green valley had lain so still
for so many centuries it seemed to us
the outstretched body of an ubiquitous god.
By evening we'd grown tired of the ruins
of France, of ourselves. On the way back
horses strode from shadows of cypress groves
to demand apples, and they too tired us. Like other
nights in the Isle de France the first years
of our marriage we spent the night in a musty hotel
ravenously eating whole chickens roasted with
Norman apples, turnips and potatoes, cream.
As if marriage itself left us starving
we made love for hours in an ancient bed
we rose from to tables the landlady set
with baskets of bread swallowed with milk
and coffee, baskets refilled and emptied
until nothing was left but the morning's fullness,
cornfields where crows cawed. In the cemetery
where Van Gogh and his brother Theo are buried
mist rose at dawn from tombstones whose inscriptions
we read again and again, yearning for more than names
and numbers in the unconjurable stone. Beyond us
husks ripened in the brilliant sun, swaying
kernels of new corn soon skimmed by waiting
blackbirds, patient wings indifferent to our need.

TREE LINE

Fifteen hundred feet above the Gorges du Tarn,
the huge, fragrant trees stopped hovering over us
like a compact, its fine print
of honeysuckle that went up in flames
of wildfire the following summer. That summer
as we rode our bicycles around hairpin curves,
only a few twigs of brush tumbled and burned
to ash in the road, small fires that came
from nowhere, led to nothing. Thankful
to reach the tree line where there was
nothing to burn, we rode mile
after mile over unseen rivers, water
dripping through chalk, the plateau
called Causse Noire, whose water
is too deep in the bones, whose water
has the inevitability of a solitude
that fails. In a landscape like that
even long marriage is like the three thousand
canvases of an old master that will burn like a forest
of old dry fir. Finding no campground,
no hotel, we trespassed into a clearing
surrounded by thorny brush, so alone
in a place human beings have lived so long
it needed no fences to tell us we weren't
wanted. There, we built our own fire,
a puff of air among stars, a dense blanket
of light that smothered speech. Once
in the night we both woke, felt the weight
of possibility slip from us like a river
through chalk.

CHANCE

If it wasn't for the train I had to listen
for from the kitchen window and the money
we fought about all night, I'd have stayed longer
in bed, the man I married
asleep beside me. Instead, all winter,
I grabbed a peach scarf and ran
in the rain up the steps of the quai
and into a blue train, just as the doors shut,
stumbling. I was always stumbling
when I belonged to childhood the way someone who's never left home
belongs to one country, one town, one family. I had to change twice
on the way to work, to the job I found through the temp agency,
where I sat all day in a small room with a window overlooking
the Seine, and my bosses both chain-smoked American cigarettes.
The older one watched me as if I were the sun that I never saw shine
and once said "You Americans know nothing
of pain, nothing of your enormous good luck,"
so that I laughed and took years to figure out
how much I hated partial truths, the river, the telephone
I answered in the smoky office, or why once
before I took dictation my boss spread his fifteen passports
like a deck of cards across his desk. Like all the other vacancies
I filled on short notice, called like a doctor to a high-risk delivery
in the early hours of the morning, that labor
lasted too long: an entire winter waiting for connections
on the platform in Courbevoie watching the fog roll in,
feeling sick about how much I wanted
the American I met once a week
at his apartment when his wife was gone
that year when, like a child or the friends
who called from America, I still believed in my own good luck.

THE DEVIL'S HOUR

Just inside the gates of the park
was a little bluff below which suburban houses
were stacked like bibelots from the Limoges museum
across the shelves of hillside streets towards a vanishing point
that held up the horizon of black glass skyscrapers of La Défense,
gigantic mirrors that reflected their mirage of power
too far off for us to see. Even after the divorce
nothing could stop us from meeting in the park of Saint-Cloud,
on ground whose name we translated as dream,
to watch Paris from the bluff before we entered
the boxwood labyrinth where we stretched and wrestled
and where once, after you'd already married someone else,
before we ran through the park
were silly enough to make love in the labyrinth and no one saw
though they might have seen
that when we stepped into the alley of old, old oak,
when we skirted the terrace with its stones from ruins of the castle,
we were innocent enough to be weeping,
knew enough to keep on running, clothes soaked,
inhaling the odor of rotting leaves, the wet trunks of trees,
running five miles through the thickets and into the open. Season
after season after we separated we couldn't stop
running together, the last bit of our marriage
we held onto. Even after we'd given up the tea we drank
in china cups your aunt brought back from England,
the faded blue wallpaper, the kitchen table,
we kept meeting in the park. I remember
when we still shared the same bed,
I read you Pessoa's *The Devil's Hour*. Pessoa knew
how the devil loves a domestic scene,
how the transcendent ruins everything it yearns for
by subtraction. At the end
we both had children, other people, new lives. All that
was left of our marriage were the skyscrapers
and the sky, which belong
to the devil, who has nothing.

TACT

"Everyone's mocking me," Anne-Marie screamed
at Sebastian. A man's hand broke something. No child,
I did what a child does, pressed my face to the window,
tried not to hear that things crashed and shook,
then, comforted by the taste of dust, remembered
the possibility of escape in sunlight, the veranda
that faced the swampy field where a herd of small, black
Camargue bulls had capered behind a stone wall
for five hundred years. Listening
to the bellowing, drinking kir, I knew the sound
of an angry animal was better than a human being
cursing behind closed doors. The fury
behind the bedroom door of the farmhouse
was like any inexplicable fury, like the rages
of my parents who fought for hours, like most couples,
behind shut doors. Years since childhood,
I know it's laughable to think wooden doors
can keep a child from hearing the thunder
of a man throwing a grown woman from the bed
to the floor in the early hours of the morning,
or that walls are thick enough to muffle the howling
of a man who's just had a woman spit in his face, so that,
mercifully, instead of hitting her, he
smashes his fist through a glass window. Anyone
would know what Sebastian and Anne-Marie sounded like
if as a child he'd heard his parents accuse, weep,
make love toward dawn while every child in the house
lay in bed, eyes open, wondering. Like
my own parents, who stunned me morning after morning
by laughing when I asked when the divorce
would be, smirking at each other as if the night
were a private joke to shatter children, the friends
of my early adulthood smiled the smile which had ceased
to astonish me; at dusk they joined us as usual
on the veranda, holding hands. We drank pastis,
kir, strong, sweet drinks. Looking out

at that ancient swamp, the Camargue, we listened
in mock horror to the story of how the bulls
would escape the walls at night in search of cows,
and, finding none, fight each other in the moonlight, ram
the farmhouse where adults slept and children pretended
to sleep.

RAIN

It's a good place to sleep,
the stubble-filled plain between arid peaks
above which, if you're not lucky enough
to sleep there on one of the rare days
it rains, you'll see stars that might keep you awake
for the rest of your life, marveling
at your own brevity, at the illusion
of length so elegantly wrought by your birth
beneath the nonerogenous stars. Nothing is
erotic beneath the peaks of Peyrepertuse,
especially if it was pouring rain
all afternoon as you pedaled hard up a mountain.
With your lover you wandered through the foundation
of the failed fortress, saw, not ghosts, but worse,
infinitely older: the memory of the Cathars
who came to the bluff overlooking the plain
knowing they were nothing to the ones
that mattered. It's hard to sleep in a place

like that, where peace isn't born
sobbing like a baby from suffering, but
of the seven hundred years of silence that came after
the Crusaders who left nothing because the powerful
care mostly for their own mysteries, not the terrors
of the untillable soil from which the Cathars made
music, poetry, grace, which, nevertheless
didn't keep them from dying or keep the fortress
from being in a land so arid, so harsh, it's still
in the middle of nowhere, so that all that's left
seven hundred years later are stones you and your lover
kick aside to make a smooth place to sleep,
a place you hope won't hurt you much, that won't
cut your knees when you lie down to make love
until you're bleeding beneath the rare sky
from which rain is mercifully falling.

ORIFLAMME

Nap as dull and worn as rock
it shed its passionate story,
the crewel stitch, worsted thread
once thick as bluegrass,
now drawn thin through yellowing linen,
the brilliant colors of mythical
birds and beasts, of wounded green
horses and blue men
fading to become again
natural things, without narrative,
like sand or the waves on the beach
we walked down earlier,
bending over, man and wife,
to search through kelp
for beige winkles no longer filled
with animals squirming like the plots
of unfinished anecdotes. The Bayeux
Tapestry unfurled like a nautilus
from the pliable hands that made it
a thousand years ago,
down the dim lit hallways
of the museum, like the unfolding
arc of a prayer, like the tree
of liberty whose roots crawled,
polished black sea turtles,
a hundred feet above ground
toward the entrance of the museum.
The warp and woof of the northern
landscape twisted its way into
our young marriage as if we were pulp. Ten years
after contemplating the fragility
of the needlepoint homage
to double invasions
I see us clearly,
hand in hand, in the same
preservative light, examining
the hopeful banner of a threadbare story.

EXPRESS

For years those hours, elbows propped
   on marble tabletops were my life. That,
and waiting for the white porcelain cup
   to arrive. Accompanied by clowns
in yellow parachute silks, black and white
   mimes I threw change to. Almost always
while I waited in chill cafés that reeked
   of smoke a man, usually my husband,
squandered his own time at another café
   waiting for me to show up. Each of us
would drink coffee and think about God,
   a bad play, but that's what we did:
drink coffee and watch the pigeons,
   thousands of them, blown off the fountain
of Saint-Sulpice by a terrible wind.

THE FARMHOUSE

For years before the damage
was covered by a roof they slept sheltered
from wind, but not from rain, not from starlight.
But it was summer twenty years ago Jaques and Danielle
finished the job, so that by the time
we knew them we could eat and drink
in a room smelling of new pine, at a table
of freshly split oak, where for hours we tore
leaves off chestnuts, threw twigs into the fire,
talked about French politics, deconstructionism,
Chateaubriand, anything just to be talking,
for in that house I learned to speak
again, learned the goodness of French,
of the immense and varied kindnesses necessary
for language. Tired of talking,
some afternoons when the wind and rain
slowed to a fine drizzle, we rode our bicycles
to Saint-Malo, a sea town with a wall
around it. A wall with its work to do, the seawall
of Saint-Malo protects it now
from waves and wind, once kept out bands
of marauding pirates. With the other tourists
we walked through the narrow, cobbled streets,
knowing what others have known, that it's a fine thing
to drink clear, cold cider, eat buckwheat
pancakes on a rainy day within the walls
of Saint-Malo, and, later, to see the men coming back
in their tattered fishing boats, slinging
nets full of crab onto the dock
while we watched from the jetty. Once,
we walked far out on the seawall,
came back to a farmhouse by way of a road
that led past the sunken lanes of Brittany, bulldozed
to join field to field. Like ruined pastures,
long conversation, houses fall again, the familiar
heaviness of abandonment signaling the end
of labor comes, then the sweet, sweet smell
of apples fallen near the mantel, then autumn
light, clear and intoxicating as cider
pouring onto summer's last unmown grass.

GHOSTS

Books haunted your house like ghosts.
I knelt before shelves of Gallimard
editions, prisoners behind
doors with elaborate scrollwork, tiny
bronze keys. I'd open a cage and vellum
fell out like the bones and feathers
of trapped animals, the thick pages
uncut. Even with your family gone
for the summer, with you gone
to another country, I stayed
loving the house and its unread walls
of books, the best place
I ever found for reading, that house
I was afraid of losing. That I lost
when you came home from your new life
in the middle of the night, and I
was reading Eluard in bed, flat
on my back, naked in the awful
August heat, the book of elegies
held high, casting its shadow
across my belly. Too suddenly
you leaned over me. I drew
the pages down, pressed words
to my skin like a cotton
shirt, a thing light
as gauze to cover me.

LAVENDER HONEY

Beneath the arbor of white grapes
we'd dropped passion or pretense
of passion, our only labor pinching lavender
buds from the stalk, dropping them grain
by fragrant, inedible grain into white
porcelain bowls. Too comfortable to make love
after breakfast we bathed in the cistern, napped
afternoons, covered with cotton sheets billowing
like drifts of sand beneath the ceiling fan, our
bodies beautiful in the ways that the hills
above Nice were beautiful, useless and shimmering
in August heat. Only once, growing impatient
with what we called "our mutual lethargy,"
we pedaled hard twenty miles up the mountain
to a walled city outside which the only trees
were the solemn cypresses, and olive trees
like commandments, stern and purposeful trees
that frightened us. Entering the city streets,
we found what we'd come for, lavender honey
thick as butter, a sugar gathered drop by drop
harvested by patient keepers. We took the honey back
to our pink house. In the back garden
figs split open on the trees were filled
with ants like tiny black seeds, with wasps
crazy in love with juice oozing from the wound
they burrowed into fruit. I took four figs,
washed them with water that poured from a stone
lion's head through a pipe plunged straight
into the side of the mountain. In the blue dusk,
we ate figs, goat cheese, lavender honey,
drank pale wine with cassis we sipped undiluted, the hollow
of the waning moon tilted above us like a silver spoon.

AFFINITIES

During the lunchtime lecture
on Goethe, the slide carousel spun
the mystical spectrum on and off
the auditorium's white screen. Infinity was
somewhere inside me, and I was sunk deep
into an upholstered chair, half-listening, half-remembering
how that morning you'd slammed the car door
in my face, pulled out of the garage
into the streets of Paris, leaving tracks
in new-fallen snow. That departure
was a canvas so stark, so blank, I didn't believe
anyone's theory of color could fill it.
The expert began to explain
to us—a group of men and women with nothing
to do at lunchtime but listen to Goethe's
theory of elective affinities—
how bodies attract and repulse
through chemistry. Then my body became
an impossible earthly thing, pool of iron-
red water. I couldn't get away fast enough, couldn't leave
the Musée d'Art Moderne fast enough. Not wanting
to see the neat blocks of brilliance
that lined the walls that winter, I ran
down the escalator past Klee's Mediterranean
landscapes, past the harmonic cubism
of the Delaunays, Franz Marc's bright green
sleeping dog that accepted everything
into the street as starkly black
and white as the last canvases of Modrian.

TRINITÉ

For years I walked past the stone
church of Trinité as if it wasn't there,
as if the quarried rock were the mountainous ghost
of a belief the past had conjured into December
air. A fortress kept out the living, garrison
of unkempt roses, damp benches covered
in green mold, a courtyard
always occupied by men in rotting clothes.
For years I hardly saw stones,
roses, bums. Summer or winter,
if I lingered on my way to the Gare
Saint-Lazare I preferred to watch
the woman who sold mandolins
beneath the Galeries Lafayette awnings,
who took buckets full of living things—
red peppers, turnips, apples, cheese—
turned them into confetti, bright ribbons
passed out to the crowd like armfuls
of gorgeous proof. I loved
the parade of the skeptical crowd
who accepted slices of fruit small as wafers,
who drank from juices she squeezed
from a machine. Only once, shortly
before I moved out of the house we shared
in the suburbs did I go inside
the Trinité, pushing open the weathered
wooden door, ducking beneath plastic
that kept out wind, to pay five francs
for a long, white taper to set down
with the others. Then, I don't know why,
in the winter afternoon outside,
I asked myself what I believed,
looked towards the ghost I hoped
I wouldn't see again, nodded
at the bums gathered around a trash can of fire.

AFTER CAVAFY

If love is the art
of filling up empty spaces
then the night we entered
the lonely pine cabin,
making it resonate
with music and passion,
we had a rare skill.
Do you remember
how good we were,
with what grace,
after a day of skiing
through the woods,
beneath snow-covered branches,
after a dinner of rich stew
the color of dark honey,
after the goat cheese
and wine,
we threw off our bright
woolen sweaters
and danced until
the empty space
beneath cold stars
almost caught
fire? That night
we crawled
into frozen blankets,
loving every pore
of skin, every
lonely crack
in each other's
human body. Such
was the talent
we once both possessed.

GARDEN

The nurse says
breathe. I breathe in:
Genesis. I breathe out:
Genesis: I remember

tropical hibiscus, fleshy petals,
pink-orange flags waving gaily
over the country of nowhere.
This hospital's the greenhouse
of hearts. I'm a stalk
of pleading, each cry
the alpha and the omega, green vowel,
green vowel. God,

protect this child.
This child. Take away
this pain. Don't leave me
caught in the alphabet
of the beginning and the end.

BELLEVILLE

From within the Swedish department store
I watched one swirl of people crowd
in and out of the Belleville metro station, another
that rose and fell from cafés, fragrant with coffee
and Israeli wines. I wandered among luxuries
I couldn't afford: taffy-colored porcelains,
linen table settings, bronze napkin rings.
The few things I bought were brittle
and beautiful. So once I chose
a crimson coffee cup. Once
a crystal vase. And once
coming into the street
with a set of long-stemmed wine glasses
I met a man I thought
I could love. In Belleville,
where everyone carries pink paper bags
filled with breakable toys, and young girls
walk out of Tati's with their wedding dresses
spilling like cream onto the hopeful pavement,
I began talking to a young actor
who took me home to meet
his girlfriend and his cat. The next morning
we woke, all of us, in the same bed, drank milk
with raspberry syrup from one of the few things
I managed to carry, years later, all the way
back to America without breaking.

II

SHELTER

Fine red mist on the Smokey Mountains.
I eat oatmeal in the foothills, indebted
to the eaves of my small house
beneath which I read Sappho, scatter pecans
with bare, chilled toes, kicking shells
across the profusion of scattered leaves. At last
comfortable enough to be grateful

to two strangers, Hasidic Jews
who once invited me to live
with them for free
my last month in Paris. From a distance
of three years, three thousand miles,
I thank them. Without ceremony,
with my small daughter for companion,
I left Europe. Leaving their
apartment, I saw rain
falling onto the cracked sidewalk,
fluorescent lights beneath green art
deco arches of the Metro
shining from below. And now I remember

one autumn in the Blue Ridge
when I was twenty-three, I slept
in a tent of fine mesh. Beside me
someone whose body was radiant
as the starlight I watched, open-eyed,
all night. For myself alone, perhaps,
I can say the failure of presence
has been the strangest
of gifts. This morning,
after driving my daughter to school,
I come home, watch the ghost
of mountains glitter on the horizon,
torn, red silk.

FOIL

In the Alcoa city park, men roll
a mower across trillium. All spring
I laugh at myself for teaching
the beauty of language to anyone
who inhales this same rare odor
of forest violets sliced beneath a mower
driven by men who work when they can. All
spring I meet the aluminum plant retiree
who, the sharp cold of winter crumpled,
parades his hands, misshapen monuments,
around the park, gloves pulled off
to unveil fingers like shattered clay
he holds towards me in disbelief
asking how am I supposed to work
with hands like these? His hands,
cracked and knobby as the trunk
of a dogwood tree, twisted sheets of aluminum
onto tubes of cardboard for forty years,
diaphanous element he held like a wife
whose ghost-like presence still shines
in his hands as he watches the factory
spit smoke into a field of Black Angus
and goldenrod. "We'd make it into jewels,"
he says of the once semi-precious stuff
that cast his body like sprung rhythm,
his hands like crushed foil, the grandeur
in his palms shaking like flame or a broken heart.

WILL-O'-THE -WISP

Swerving
around a bird that pecks at a luscious-looking rotten apple
in the middle of the right lane, I wish I knew

an answer better than silence to the dazzle of these redbuds,
azaleas, pools of water. My meditation
is a strange plume in the brilliance of spring, the surprise

of fluttering leaves on uncut timber in the backwoods
spangled by my thoughtfulness
like the red squirrel whose dazzling guts sparkle on the road like rubies.

The squirrel vanishes like fallen leaves, like my own loves,
like my daughter's childhood, which I love, like all the life I'll ever know,
too briefly to answer. I think that I know nothing,

that my knowledge
is no different from the flaming azalea bushes
among the redbuds and dogwoods, that all I ever want life to know

I'd be able to say that swiftly. This morning my daughter
woke before me and came to sit in the dark
of the room where I was still sleeping.

When I opened my eyes, she was sitting on the white sofa
looking straight at me, waiting. As if wanting more from me
than breakfast or cartoons, her face was lit up

and the life in her blue eyes
was a blessing like fire on water
coming towards me from the shadows.

ASHES

When I see the ash trees next to the red earth
of the new riverfront development and the bulldozer
bow in the wind over and over
as if asking forgiveness, I stop the car
knowing beauty needs me to indulge
its pointless sublimity. It was in Paris
that I first learned what it was to live
without beauty. Angry and poor,
I wandered through bright museums
on weekends, so tired from making money
I'd sit for hours in front of smoky canvases
of Saint-Lazare hoping for the miracle
of feeling. Have you ever
walked into a synagogue as I did
one Yom Kippur to sit on the balcony
in the women's section watching
men covered in white shawls
pray, like a thicket of ash trees
spared by the storm? Have you ever
been without compassion
for the prayers of men? If you have
ever felt as I did, balefire banked
by ashes of bitterness and grief,
you understand why I write this poem
to bless all that's ever risen
from beauty's pale soot.

PINK PETUNIA

Again through ash and soil,
feeling to the bottom for fine white roots
I pinch clumps from plastic pots to set
wilting stems, devastating blossoms
into each row of hollows I fill, cover,
until the bones of my fingers ache from grasping
small, bright flowers. Fine work for sundown
which is happening behind the dogwood
beneath which my daughter reads
a book about dinosaurs, feet propped
on a plastic table: "Did you know
in two thousand years everything alive
on earth will be dead?" Palms open,
she accuses my petunias, then sweeps arms
wide to include the bird feeder—the jays
fighting off red-winged blackbirds, a couple
of mourning doves below. Her gaze is the level,
calm gaze of the serious child who wants
no frivolous comforting, not this child
whose first words—"the moon, the moon"—
comforted me, so for a little while
I laughed at the impermanence of all
identity. Not Justina, who looks down, intones
in the hymn-like voice of the new
reader: "The flower
appeared at the end of the Jurassic Era."

HOLLYHOCKS

Old-fashioned hollyhocks still astonish the sun
whose light gasps the whole world forth. I go
to see new blossoms in dawn mist like breath,
see-through collages of bright scraps of paper.

Children gasp, laughing, separate worlds when I go
to collect my daughter from summer camp
where she's made a see-through collage of bright paper.
Children make astonishing flowers with their hands

that parents take home with their children.
I hang paper flowers in the house when I'm afraid.
Children make beautiful art with their hands
though the test results come back positive.

I hang them in the house where I'm afraid,
with blossoms of flowers, fruit of my child's hands.
Test results come back positive; it's commonplace
as saying death stops for one thing at a time,

first the blossoms of flowers, then children's hands.
Astonishing hollyhocks outgrow the sun. Old-fashioned,
we gasp, "mortality's the gardener that touches us, one
by one, to see new blossoms in dawn mist like breath."

BURNING WATER

This Tennessee summer stretches past
October, yearns towards the first week
of the eleventh month like the warm grasp
of a newborn ghost extended to feel
autumn fruit: acorns, persimmons, the last
pears that drop from branches of turning leaves.
The fruit's the speech of the green mirage
that rippled above us all summer; the broken seal
between air and pith; the soul of summer unfastened
into the tongue of fruit. Generations have sung
this flame red rain sluicing the viaduct
of blue to Earth's cistern, the infinite
basin of rich decay, the burning dung
each rain-dampened, trampled leaf has struck.

HORSES

They bloom in May pastures
like flowers, their tangled manes
blowing in the wind, catching on the fence posts.
They wander, muzzles to the ground, sputtering and snorting.
Their bodies shine. Their bellies

are swollen with clover and milk.
Beneath the shadow of a tree,
the foals prance on spindly legs
like sticks of hard candy.

When did we forget
their thrilling bodies?
The smell of pastures, oats and dust
was the first passion we knew
for what moves beyond us. A herd of mares

camped our bloodstream. We rode them out
of ancient civilizations,
building new cities, galloping
an alphabet now become obsolete. Children,
we still knew what it was like
to need horses, to learn the steady blessing
of their solemn breath was what exhaled the impossible,
light flicker of their heavy necks in play. We studied
our own stillness beside their nervous, twitching flanks.

We learned to love horses as we learned to read,
brushing our curry combs over winter coats
rough with mud as consonants, picking the round hooves
clean as vowels, making the entire warm body
of their otherness grunt with pleasure, making them shine
with their original brightness.

CYPRESS

My family faced cool cypresses, privacy
of charcoal, of meat spitting on the grill,
protected by shadows, brick wall
of good times, mortar of russet potatoes
wrapped in foil, thud of steak on porcelain,
paradise of golden oil, of silvery butter,
communion of fragrant basil, of pale honeysuckle
blossoming in afternoon heat. We licked
the salt from our bare hands, belief, warm
and sweet as corn on the cob. That July fourth
on my sister's pine sun deck, my father's
death waited four months ahead like a star's
implosion, distant, cold, easily dwarfed
by the children's sparklers in the blue dusk.

SYMMETRY

As long as nature keeps popping up with its embarrassing
array of gorgeous theorems—the flock of cardinals
that collided in mid-air with a golden finch, the double
rainbow which I might have prevented
from astonishing me had it not been reflected
in the pale brick of the building opposite
when the rainbow arched over Paris—

I'll have to keep reminding myself that the past,
like any logician's proof, has dismantled
the argument by design. What a waste that the sun
persists in breaking through steel-gray clouds
to shine on the mountaintops of the Blue Ridge,
that the land stubbornly remains
naive, landscape done by a painter of the Hudson River
school, after all the twentieth century

has shown us, our recent past that most awesome Houdini
of human vanishing. Too bad a magician must leave
all props behind, ours being almost too terrible
to name: camps, candles lit in six million names,
and after that, more to come, governments
like the black cloak the magician draped over a table,
memorials of black stone. Magic, once a candle flame,

roared through our lives like wildfire. Is beauty
then beside the point? Precursor of nothing?
Perhaps. What to make of it? Once I rode
a silver horse through the charred hills
above Nice to a vineyard bordered by olive trees
untouched by fire. Among thousands of ruined acres,
one family had begun to prepare for the harvest. Selfish?
Perhaps. But the women went on setting up tents for shelter

in an olive grove ancient and human as a ruined coliseum.

THAW

Yesterday's snow melts into red clay,
cushions hollows once plumbed
by the cabling roots of long-eroded
trees. Both roots and branches
pierce the pond's surface now
with the silver flicker of driftwood.
From earth to bare upper branches
warblers flit. Purple stalks
shine among grey twigs, beige rushes,
all the lushness of summer sucked
through winter's dry straw
back to the pond of green water, leaf
by red leaf by gold leaf by leaf rot
deliquesced from shape to ripple,
no matter how those shapes sustained
us with beloved presence. No matter

how dangerously close to meaning
the fallen, snow cradles the brittle
twigs. Cells built flake
by white flake into muscular drifts
melt. A dream of last summer's leaves
lays gauzy as green moss spores
over the icy mud, memory
the body's struggle to make
something of vanishing: from
Chattanooga's wooden pedestrian bridge
your pleasure in the familiar water
surged like the river that cuts through
Alabama, doubles back into Tennessee
before disappearing into the Mississippi. We
made a wish for the river at a well that sucked
our bright copper penny into a spinning vertex.
We wished the river well and walked away
from water so incomprehensible
I can only say it betrays us, we
who ask where summer has gone,
ourselves the snows of yesteryear.

INTERVAL

The cicadas sing on the first night
my daughter spends away from home,
dark animal throb accompanying me
from room to room. It's been a long time

since light has fallen over the emptiness
of the room where beauty comes
and goes, comes and goes because the night
is full of responsibility I can't refuse

when dreamless I waken to the sound of breath
in the little room where toy horses
prance behind the nightlight,
their real silver manes ready for brushing.

HYPOTHESIS

The clouds flame,
great, golden bodies brought to life
by chance wind, moonlight. So, too,
memory flares through the lives of the dead:
my father's hands cradling a cup of tea
as he helps with my geometry homework
brush my arm, warm and flexible.
He sets down his favorite cup,
scribbles the proof to my hypothesis
easily as any master draftsman might
correct the error in a student composition.
He picks up the brown cup and blows,
his living lips pursed, his living breath
cooling the steaming tea. My father
lies in the final, intimate space, his passion
for mathematics, his body, vanished. Overhead,
cloud banks thicken, grown flat, impercipient.
No wonder moonlight makes me weep.

TELL ME WHAT THE WORLD IS LIKE

Tell me what the world is like,
bring the horizon close,
make the squirrel be still,
and I'll take you to the beautiful place

you're afraid of, show you
the tiny animal
that never sleeps. Mama,
look at me a long time,

make me a promise
that shines
like the tip
of a wing, and I'll give you

a thing that has never been,
that blossoms
from the invisible seed
that needs

so much to live
it feeds off the earth,
the black mulch, the harvest
your own mother named nothing.

PARADISE

I take in the ribs of the winnowing
machine, its rusted bones indistinguishable
from red clay; look through the sockets
of shadow that were windows, to haystacks
covered in black mold. I walk

down the gravel road through the deserted city
of the dairy, its barn one of the ruined castles
of America. I sightsee the imaginary glory
of milk, calcium ghost in a rubble of hewn
stone, then move up the hill to the ridge

where the sky preaches its elegy of red brimstone
to the interstate below, to headlights, uncomprehending
as new stars in the early dusk. High
above the dairy I smell horses,

mortal, unmoving, blanketed bodies
heavy as boulders, snorting and nuzzling
the fence as I pass. A blue car, emblem
of the city police emblazoned on its side,
stops beside me. The young officer rolls
down his window, unfolds a map. I thank him,
and walk in the direction he shows me

to a valley like a goblet of the last light
of this year. In the sloping meadow,
a herd of deer grazing on frozen grass
sees me. White tails unfurl. More like wings than flags.

SONG

Let all comfort creep
Through earth and grass,
The heron's majestic flight
End with a graceless splash

In still water, rattling husks
Of cream-colored wheat bow
And scatter. No loftiness
Should silence us. Let the West

Virginia mountain peaks crumble
Like granite idols to Kentucky valleys,
The grandeur of the sun trickle
To sparkle on a sip of water. Let

Prayers of grief be earthbound,
Etched in calcified bone
Like the whorl of shells, hidden
As spider webs in musty barns,

Croak from the throat of a frog
Big as my thumb, damp skin brown
As tree bark, twang rising
Like heaven from the roots of pine.

III

EXPLOSION

Scrub pine jagged as blue granite
pebbles the rough skin of Appalachian
mountains. Unfamiliar West Virginia
startles me from daydream long enough to see
a bright yellow finch dart through weeds
on the shoulder. Then, I dream again: one
by one the bodies of those I love extinguished
like blown glass, center collapsed,
pitched back into the fire. In an instant
the world held inside my father's body
implodes, cerulean blue explosion
of Murano glass, the landscape that lived
inside him scattered like a confetti
of blue flowers. Years ago my father
drove this same road through West Virginia
towards the Kentucky hills. Did he
too see the earth unfold towards the Ohio,
petal of brilliant blue horizon opening
on blue petal to the river's flesh at its center?
      That world's still here this August morning.
I fly across state lines as if in dream,
each exit the escape route to another town's
grief. I drive, dreaming, until, shifting
lanes across the river, I almost kill
a motorcyclist dressed in black. Thanking
God I didn't send him, broken black mirror,
into the Ohio River, I slow, and the cyclist
roars past me screaming obscenities. The world
is never what we want, won't let us be
lost, which is what we want, mostly.
A merciful roughness leads us from our grief
to gravel paths where heat like raw silk
wrestles with insects, where in the confusion
of crown vetch and Queen Anne's Lace we stumble
down to the water's edge, let ourselves fall
with relief at having hurt no one in our sleep.

WELCOME CENTER

Just the other side of the Tennessee state line
where a ragged blue sign tells us we've crossed
the border from Kentucky, on the Cumberland
Plateau, warblers flit along split rails
skirted by goldenrod and cornflowers, a garden
near the women's restroom, a threshold of roaring
motorcycles, happy dogs, whining children.
All the month of August, I've driven across
the South, from Maryland to West Virginia
mountains down through Kentucky to Tennessee
for this, for rest areas off the highway, for
any Motel 6, anywhere I could alight
on the world as if it were a fence post,
a place I could perch in the infinite
space of my father's death. The last day of his life
a bird black as my father's eyes flew into my body
as I led him from the couch back to bed.
Hours earlier, the hospice nurse had told us
his breath had "the fruity smell of the dead."
That night he spat blood. Between forgetting
and remembering the black bird flies. Once
at a birthday party, my father inserted
batteries into a kind of furry, pink monster,
made the toy work, so that we howled with laughter
when the creature gave birth to a large, blue egg.
Memory's a blue weed, a cornflower, that battered,
blue roadside banner. I cling to the tattered
edges, to the hand dryer's broken wheezing
in the women's bathroom. To a goldfinch feeder
that almost blots out the interstate. Cars rush
in glittering rows, vanish over the horizon. Near rest
areas, goldfinches bicker among ornamental grasses,
struggle for thistle seed, eat fast, flutter off,
their uncertain flight the lesser gaiety that salutes us.

FRUIT

Brevity is the peach
the sun-burnt woman slices with a knife
she plunges to the hard pit of fruit
she holds out to us, so that we taste
how good it is, and the chins of the children
drip. At the fruit stand,
I rub the blood-red core of the peach.
As if its juice were tears, I remember days

when life has been a prayer
to leave the fruit
in the wooden bowl
untouched. It's the same choice
driving home through blue mountains,
and I could drive straight through
until the horizon becomes familiar, disappears
into close-upness of grass and pine. This time

I stop the car and look and look,
letting the distance become strange,
letting my life become empty and pure
as a stranger's, unknown, without memory
to lengthen it, until I almost believe
decision's tiniest seeds
had never grown into fruit. Until
my six-year-old daughter whispers,

"It's so beautiful here."

BLACKBERRIES

In Champagne at the family mansion, random
  pebbles crunched like bits of luck beneath
my boots. I was a woman, my freedom
  brief. My child slept in her wicker basket
beneath the oak board where friends kept watch
  and played cards for high stakes, a game
too serious for me, casual player
  who enraged them. Instead of playing
I walked into the woods dusk filled
  like an artery pumping its deep blue light
from the stone house that stood on the horizon
  like a heart. I knew then the universe
would take me no farther than the bare
  brambles that each summer filled with black fruit.

INFINITY

Beyond the streetlamps
burned the sky I'd seen the summer before
when the odor of rosemary and lavender
flared, scent that seemed a flame
the stars exhaled upon Earth. The fire-
breathing loveliness of the world. . . If it's true,
as you said, that losing a leg
singes worse than losing a lover, it's also true
I slapped you for saying it. Day after day
I looked for a form
that would make grief less
beautiful. I took the train to Nanterre,
wandered the hallways of the stone university,
attended a seminar on Milton. All winter,
I grew thin eating apples, but the beauty
so close to the original brightness
wouldn't leave me. Instead, black ink,
gorgeous as the portrait Milton paints
of hell, burned, each letter a red-hot coal
of speaking, white space like Mediterranean
sunlight sparking the forest
of awe inside me, tall, dark trees
set alight by the alphabet. Meanwhile,
bums warmed themselves by the garbage can
of fire outside, and you lived in Berlin
with another woman. Nights, I sat in the bedroom
we'd papered ourselves, listening to Emmy Lou Harris,
the music of Iraqui mystics, watching moths
flutter about the halogen lamp. When the music
stopped, there was the gentle burning of the animal
that gets too close to the fire.

CONVERSATION

When I lacked compassion
I'd look out the floor-to-ceiling windows
of the language school near the Madelaine
to a courtyard filled with flowers. Then,
I could listen again
to the terrible stories my students told me
as if broken hearts could mend
fractured syntax. At twenty-three
I was learning the seed
that people want most
to plant in the furrows
of a strange tongue
is what hurts: the secretary
and her migraines, the executive
and her fall, eight months pregnant
on some steps in Montmartre,
the mother in advanced beginning
and her son, practically psychotic
from unrequited love, who took
intermediate conversation. I
tried to look dispassionate,
commented on sentence structure,
vocabulary. The students
listened to my grammar
suggestions seriously.
As if the child I was
could give them what they wanted
week after week, they memorized
English verb tenses that took root
then blossomed slowly as orchids
on tongues of dense earth.

UNIVERSAL

During the separation,
each time I hung up the phone
the silence in the house,
a pinprick of darkness
heavy as the original world,
exploded to the far edges
of an expanding galaxy.
My voice was so many stars
that wandered these heavens,
disappeared. Until, exhausted,
I began to hear the ghost of things
speak back to me: summer's
first peaches ripening on the sill,
a split, black plum covered in wasps,
a creamy, yellow rose tinged with blush
in the Jardin des Bagatelles,
red peonies drooping from a bush
of glossy, dark leaves. Stunned
by the universal speech of things,
I listened, passed the solstice
with a dictionary of symbols
spread on a white linen tablecloth
strewn with crystal and silver,
interpretation and thing glittering
in moonlight. Later, in an airport
in Charlotte, North Carolina, I saw
crepe myrtle planted beside the runway,
long ropes of familiar kudzu. It was
after the divorce in the airport
I heard two women speak of the beauty
of yellow roses tinged pink, and knew
the flower they spoke of, the words
that fell like stones through limpid pools
for themselves alone.

SUMMONS

During the worst of February
I'd walk away from the hospital's
busy whir, its gossip of the body,
through the new architecture of the twentieth
arrondissement, past the bluffs, their ghostly
horizons, to the Buttes-Chaumont,
where the banks of a man-made pond,
muddy with footsteps, were scattered
with chunks of bread. I'd pick up
the soggy half-loaves,
throw them back into the water
to a white swan that swam towards me,
ruffling the huge span of its wings,
hissing its hunger
as if it had been summoned like the holiness
of words read aloud from rain, from the fluttering
pages of the world's prayer book. I transliterated
hope from white quills. Later,
unmindful of symbolism,
I wrapped a black wool cardigan
around my baby—due in March,
born under three pounds
in December, brought home
in April. Done with heaven's reports
I protected her from spring wind.
Her down-covered fontanel
brushed against my chin. I wore
her timeless human weight like a second skin.

SYNAPSE

The heron perched on the snowpack an hour
while I thought my way, I thought, past folded
wings, imagined my self scrutinizing the glare
of sun, illusion that snapped like a tangled
string when the annoyed bird's flight ripped air.
I was no fisher, only myself, calm mangled
by jobs, bills, lover, child, no more aware
of the interior of a heron than capable
of living the lives of people I loved.
I never ordered the heron to glide away
or the people to freely come and go. Never.
What happened was the people went, the heron flew,
and when I drew back my blue cuff, the pulse
beat within my own nerve, synapse, sinew.

SUNLIGHT

Scrabbling beneath rocks in running water,
he pried out crayfish. Summer sun beat down
on my father's neck. Years later, I smell his skin
and the meadow filled with wildflowers
we walked through on the way home. Memory
cleaves a shortcut through fields of Queen Anne's Lace
to home, where the heat of my father's love
waits for me, bitter and sweet as watercress
we comb eager fingers through, untangling,
pulling roots free of grit and stone.
Desire for them is what we owe the dead,
to lead them from the underworld of red clay
to the day when they recognized our hunger,
boiled crayfish and cress, fed us with the sun.

GHOST

Flawed like a diamond by years, transported
from his childhood home in the Bronx, then
to a suburb in Tennessee, my father's violin
disappeared, never found after his death.
But I didn't dream that afternoon the rain
tore roses from their stems, or how, after,
sweat pouring down his back, my father
gathered rose petals to scatter into red velvet
of the violin case. Ghost of all
we love tarnishes our transient beauties:
our heirloom roses, the scent of oak roots
cracking sidewalks. Feet heavy with ghosts
clinging like mud, even our children dance in the arms
of lost things they never know are gone.

LUCK

Heroine of my family's only
Holocaust story, the only one
of my grandfather's seven sisters
to stay in Europe, before they loaded you
onto the bus in northern France, you asked
to pee, and the first miracle was
they let you, the second that when
you stepped off the road to squat
between rows of bright yellow safflower,
petals fluttering like buttery flames,
you saw a bicycle laid on its side,
its spokes still turning. You saw,
also, a man kneeling down to cup
a baby hedgehog in his palm, who
with his free hand motioned you
towards the bicycle and a stone house.
That night as you slept on the floor
of the house of the kind-hearted man,
you felt something crawl under your shirt,
across your skin, your ribs, shoulder blades,
the nape of your neck, your jawbone,
and dive down into your ear. You lay
perfectly still. The next morning
when you saw the departing tracks of the bus
in the road, the feet that had searched for you
in the dust, it was as if God had chosen
to leap from the bus with you, and though
the memory of steps crossed your brain like a stroke
of good luck your whole life, you never knew
if it were man, hedgehog, or God you were hearing.

HEARTWOOD

So what if heaven never speaks?
Far worse if the squirrel's
streak beneath a rotting tree stump
to escape us, if the blue
heron's silver wings that float
from sight to the swamp's
far edge at our approach
were invisible as God. Thank God

for glimpses of the world, for lovers,
who though they leave us,
abandon us to the real,
radiant yearning for the body.
Not desire for the dazzling
imprint of the sun, but for small
splinters of ordinary being
we can trust: a cotton shirt laced
with scent, a silver hair shimmering
in the wake of a parent's body

scatter like truth through memory.
We ourselves are evidence
of the world. Solid enough
for God himself to believe in,
we burn steadily and long.

PEAR

I pat parsley damp as newly washed hair
in the dark, brush collard greens stiff
as starched black shirts, feel through the crisper
for the hard knobs of unripe pears. Among
the shadows of kitchenware, I might believe
myself still in bed, my field of view a blur
of sheets salty with sweat and tears. I woke
at four this morning to absence, a grief
too impalpable to disturb with light, padded
down the carpeted stairs to the broken refrigerator
for a D'Anjou pear. The heft of fruit relinquishes
my hands from the dark, as if heaviness
unburdens me of shadows. Back in bed, propped
against pillows, I know nothing but this
sweetness I fold into me like a faint green star.

MEMORY, MORPHINE

I treasure the sting on my cheek
from the one time my father slapped me
by mistake, in 1973. Walking through woods
covered in deep drifts of snow
in bitter cold to feed the horses,
I wore his jacket on top of mine.
He breathed out large, frozen breaths
and inhaled, loving the ozone
and the smell of tree bark so much he stumbled
against a branch that caught my cheek
so hard the scar still shows. Memory, morphine
drip that blots out more recent memory
of my father. Dying, he refused music,
books, TV, or morphine. Like a woman
who wants to be fully present
for her baby's birth, my father
longed for some memory of his death
if only in the moment after.
"Tell your sister I like to think,"
he said to me on the telephone
when our family was devising means
of making him "comfortable." The telephone
was the last thing he gave up. Until
the last afternoon, he'd raise his head
from the pillow to crack a joke
with a friend, then stare into space
for hours, shaking with silent laughter.

VESPERS

In the car, bewildered,
I could be in a carriage driving
through Delft watching sun hit
the canal, shadow of the New Church
cast into silver water, or shuffling
across sand of an indistinct harbor at sunrise,
when it dawns on me that my forehead's inches
from the windshield of a car going sixty
miles an hour in the twenty-first century
where you are not. Since your death
I've been perhaps too easily astonished,
the world full of these glorious Turner
sunsets, these intimate pulse-constructed
exteriors of Vermeer. Tonight
I park my car next to Borders, walk
into a sunset composed of optic tricks:
the trees, a woman and her glossy black lab
entering the revolving glass doors of Pet Smart,
the cars and the asphalt parking lot, all
of them, volumes of madder. All but intaglios
of your hospital bed, the oxygen
tubes, your flesh that cancer drew
awkward as any amateur ignorant of light,
your bones the black X the past cross-hatched
across this sunset. Then ash trees catch
low January sun, the pink flush
infusing the branches. The trees at the edge
of the parking lot that spreads
from Borders to Pet Smart to Home Depot
offer this evening's mystery, powerful and bright.
Even Toyotas, SUVs, Dodge
Caravans glitter eerily in the twilight.
Even the dirty snow which piles at the curb
like memory or wasted flesh waxes full
of flashing grit, of sparkling grime.

HIBISCUS

Life alone, when it happens,
isn't quick like a hummingbird
or a bee, isn't
like the animals that spread pollen,
but like sleight of hand,
like the unfolding of certain
tropical flowers. Privacy,
prehistoric root, took
a million years to blossom
before our eyes. Life is brief,
the coffee I drink hot as a temple
of baked adobe, the linoleum
floor of the kitchen cool
beneath my feet when I go back
to a bed of white feathers. Loneliness
is the idea emptiness once had
about the flower we call hibiscus.

Katherine Smith was born in California and raised in Tennessee. She received her M.F.A. from the University of Virginia. Her poems have appeared in *Poetry*, *Shenandoah*, *The Laurel Review*, *The Southern Review*, and other magazines. An essay, "The Artist as Single Mother," appeared in *Sleeping with One Eye Open: Women Writers and the Art of Survival*, edited by Marilyn Kallet and Judith Ortiz Cofer (University of Georgia, 1999). She currently teaches at Montgomery College in Maryland, where she lives with her daughter, Justina.